STARTING SCHOOL

Caryn Jenner & Arthur Robins

W
FRANKLIN WATTS
LONDON•SYDNEY

Notes for parents and carers

**Starting a new school can be daunting.
This book helps to prepare your child – and you!**

Use this book to give your child an idea of what to expect
at school. Find out what he or she is looking forward to most.
If your child is worried, point out how the children in this
book resolve difficulties. This will help boost their confidence.
Be enthusiastic about school and your child will be, too!

A few more ideas before the big day...

★ Visit the school beforehand. Try and meet the teacher
and other children in the class.

★ Have some practice runs to school in the weeks
leading up to the first day.

★ Help your child to be more independent with skills
such as using the toilet and getting dressed.

First published in 2011 by
Franklin Watts
338 Euston Road
London NW1 3BH

Franklin Watts Australia
Level 17/207 Kent Street
Sydney NSW 2000

Text © Caryn Jenner 2011
Illustration © Arthur Robins 2011

The rights of Caryn Jenner to be identified as the author and
Arthur Robins as the illustrator of this Work have been asserted
in accordance with the Copyright, Designs and Patents Act, 1988.

With thanks to Southfield Primary School and Shayne Johnson.

A CIP catalogue record for this book is available from the British Library.

ISBN: 978 1 4451 0094 4

Printed in China

Franklin Watts is a division of Hachette Children's Books,
an Hachette UK company.
www.hachette.co.uk

To Lia, my very
curious daughter – C.J.

Contents

What is school?

Lucky you!
You're starting school soon.

School is a place to learn, try new things,

and have fun!

Other children will be starting school too,
and you'll make lots of new friends.

Getting ready

In the mornings, everyone must get to school on time. Sometimes it's a rush to get ready!

I get my school clothes ready the night before. In the morning, I get dressed **quick as a flash!**

At our school we wear uniforms. Our school badge is on the sweatshirt.

7

Arriving at school

All the children must arrive by the time school starts.

We walk to school. Sometimes we have to run so we aren't late!

My friends and I take the bus to school.

My dad drives me to school. He drops me off at the school entrance where my teacher meets us.

9

Morning routine

The children know what to do when they go into school every morning. Soon, you'll learn your morning routine, too.

First, I hang my coat on my peg. The peg has my name and a picture on it.

As soon as I go into my classroom, I sit quietly in my special place on the carpet.

11

In the classroom

The classroom is full of interesting things.
What do you think you'll find in your classroom?

People at school

Everyone at school is really nice.
It's their job to help children like you.

The headteacher is in charge of the whole school.

This is my teacher. She is in charge of my class.

The caretaker looks
after the school building.

The first-aider makes
the children feel better.

Hi, Dad!

Hi, Mum!

Hi,
doughnut!

Lots of mums and dads
help out at school, too.

Around the school

School can seem like a very big place.
But after a while you'll learn your way around.

The people in the office help to organise the school. Ask them if you have any questions.

If you get lost, there's always someone around to help.

Excuse me, I can't find my class!

School toilets

If you need the toilet at school, just raise your hand and ask your teacher. Don't try to hold it in!

School rules

Everyone at school has to follow rules.
These rules make school a safe and happy place.

Raise your hand
and wait for your
turn to speak.

Do you
want a go?

Take turns
and share.

It's your school,
so keep it tidy.

LITTER

Shhhh!
Walk quietly
in the corridors.

Be kind, helpful
and polite.

Thank you.

Listen carefully so
you know what to do.

Follow directions.

**That means do what
your teacher says!**

What we learn

You'll be learning lots of new things at school. Some things might be easy-peasy, but others will be a bit harder. Just try your best.

We're learning about letters and the sounds they make.

Playtime

There's time to run around and play at school, too.

Yippee! It's playtime!

Our class plays in this playground, but the big children play over there.

If I don't know who to play with, I ask somebody if I can join their game.

25

lunchtime

Learning is hungry work, so eat a good lunch! Some children bring a packed lunch, and others have school dinners.

27

Special days

Some days at school are extra special and extra fun!

It's Book Day. I'm dressed up as my favourite book character – the Big Bad Wolf.

Nee-naw, nee-naw! The Fire Brigade is visiting our school to talk about fire safety.

Sports Day is so much fun, I don't even mind if my team doesn't win.

Oops!

Twinkle, twinkle ...

Today, our class is doing an assembly for the whole school! I hope I remember the song.

We're on a school trip today. Can you guess where we are?

Favourite things

This is what some children say about school.
Soon this will be you. Have fun!

We do lots of fun things at my school.

I'm learning to read. That's my favourite thing!

I love it when I learn to do something new. It's a brilliant feeling!

We love school!